Meditations from
The Temple Within

A Guide to Meeting
Your Angels, Spirit
Guides and Connecting
to the Voice of Your
Higher Self

Guided Meditation CD and
Journaling Workbook

by Denise Iwaniw

This book is dedicated to my Aunt Mary Lou
and the Sabo Supper Club.

Table of Contents

Introduction

Guided Meditations from The Temple Within is about Soul work. Channel-
ing these divinely inspired journeys has been the work of my Soul for many
years now. I began leading these guided meditations after some gentle prodding
from friends, and have marveled ever since at these meditations have helped so
many connect with their Angels and Guides in Spirit. More importantly, how-
ever, these works have aided people in connecting with the voice of their Higher
Self and with their Divine Purpose. They have given others renewed Hope and
rejuvenated Spirit. Ultimately, they remind us of who We Truly Are.

Whether I am speaking at a university or with clients from Japan, South
Africa, South America or Michigan, I have learned one thing from all of them.
When we give our Soul a chance to sing, it will carry us to places and to dreams
that have long awaited our arrival.

Each of these meditations has been channeled for a specific purpose.
Whether you are entering the Enchanted Forest or the Temple of the Goddess
Isis, you will be taken to a special place within yourself where the knowledge of
these places resides. You will find your self able to tap into a dimension that
seems light years away but, in all Truth, resides in your Temple Within.

Journey with me as I take you to the Crystal Castle and the Enchanted
Garden to meet your Angels and members of the Faerie Kingdom. Come with me
to Ancient Temples to meet your Spirit Guides and encounter the Goddess of
One Thousand Names, Isis. Expand your Merkabah energy field and travel to the
Orion Belt to connect to the voice of your Higher Self. Create your heart's desire
and sit beside the Brook of Angels to encounter the Angelic Realm. All of these
places are very real. They exist in a place long forgotten by our earthly selves.
Follow me as I help you remember....

Wishing you blessings on the journey,

Denise Iwaniw

Acknowledgements

Let me begin by thanking my angels on earth, Elyse Marie-LaFave and Jane Andrew Iwaniw. They've helped me remember what they have not yet forgotten: That we come from a place not far from here and yet a place that our soul longs to be. A place where angels live and faeries dance. Where we are all connected to the Source of Creation and where we shall one day return. In their eyes, I see the hope of our earthly future and the wisdom of our heavenly home. They love me in all of my eccentricity and acknowledge who I truly am.

Without my husband, Steve, none of this work would have yet come to fruition. Steven is my earthly guardian, companion on the journey and my very best friend. In this lifetime and in many others he has helped me become who I intended to be. He nudges me along, and keeps me grounded to Mother Earth. Steve is the source of my laughter. He reminds me not to get so serious that I forget to play along the way.

To my parents, Donn and Lois Cronk, thank you for always being there for me, even when you thought it was just my imagination. I now understand why I chose you to be my parents in this lifetime, and I love you, even with the frosted beehive hairdos and aqua-colored leisure suits.

To my baby brother, Tim, thank you for the gold book-signing pen that you gave me for Christmas several years ago. Along with it came all the confidence in the world that I would one day use it. It meant the world to me then and continues to mean the world to me today. It almost makes up for the time you stuck an olive up your nose when we were kids, and I was the only one you would allow to retrieve it.

I am thankful and grateful to all of the friends that have blessed my life. Mary Ann, Marietta, Mandira and Linda, thank you for encouraging me to spread my wings and for being my spiritual cheerleaders.

Thank you, Charmaine, for your gentle guidance and unending Light. Thank you, Chris, for being my sounding board and my voice of reason. Your presence in my life is a gift beyond measure.

To Keisha, Nakoma, Tai, Mingh, Arthur, Ezra, David, Enid and Enoch: Thank you for guiding me and giving me these beautiful meditations to share with my fellow travelers. Your Light is a beacon unto my Soul.

And to my students and clients, I thank you for sharing your energy, love and wisdom with me. You've taught me more about myself and the journey of Spirit than I could possibly ever teach you. You are truly a blessing.

Thank you Wendy Mersman, at Moon Designs for the gift of your artistic insight. The graphics that you have created for this project are extraordinary and speak to my very soul.

Thank you Andrew, at Audio Bay Studios for making the recording of my work fun and easy. This is just the beginning!

Finally, I offer my unending gratitude to the Editor of this work, Mary Ann Sabo. Thank you, Miriam, for your gift friendship and of the written word, which you have so freely shared with me. You are a treasure.

Love, Denise

Meditation

"Meditation is a time of quiet, when the mind is freed from its attachmen to the hysterical ravings of a world gone mad. It is a silence in which the spirit c God can enter us and work His divine alchemy upon us."

-Marianne Williamson best-selling autho

Meditation is an exercise in freeing your Mind and Spirit of clutter. Ove the course of a single day, we are bombarded by noises, images, thoughts anc feelings that can bind us. I call this Spiritual Clutter. Meditation takes us beyonc our Physical Self to tap into that which lies within us, in our Spiritual Self.

Use this CD and Journaling Workbook as a fun tool for self-discovery. By recording your experiences and thoughts in the Journaling Workbook, you wil begin to see a side of your inner life that has always been there, just waiting to for you tap into it.

As you listen to my meditations, go easy on yourself. Do not be bothered i your mind wanders and your body resists relaxation at first. As you continue to experience these guided meditations, your body and mind will begin to gently follow your Spirit's lead.

While some people meditate in designated meditation rooms on desig-nated meditation mats called zafus, others meditate in the bathtub or out in Mother Nature. Whether you are sitting under a full moon, on the beach or lying on a sofa, the key is to be comfortable. To enhance the meditation experience, many people burn a small amount of incense before proceeding and then light a candle. Remember to ask your Angels and Spirit Guides to be with you during these meditations. Keep your breathing simple, inhaling through your nose and exhaling through your mouth. Continue to do this throughout the meditation. It's just that easy.

After listening to a meditation, open your Workbook to the written version of what you have just heard. It is not necessary to follow along. At the end of each meditation you will find question and answer pages. Write everything that you felt, heard or saw during the journey. Don't edit anything, simply let the words flow through your hand. Remember that Angels and Guides in Spirit come to people in many different shapes and forms. While some may take a human form, others appear as pure light. Because we are all different, we will experi-ence things differently as well. There is no wrong or right way to see, hear or feel these meditations. They have been given to you to experience Spirit as only your Soul can.

Meeting Your Angels
-the Crystal Castle

The purpose of this guided meditation is to connect with your Guardian Angel(s) as you journey into The Crystal Castle. Our Angels walk with us during our lifetime to help us accomplish our Soul's True Purpose. Some of our Angels remain with us throughout our lifetime; some come into our lives to help us accomplish a specific task. This meditation will lead you to the Angel or Angels who are working with you during this period of your spiritual Journey.

Meditation: Breathe deeply through your nose. And as you do, settle comfortably into your surroundings. Exhale through your mouth, and send away all worries, concerns and distractions. Breathe deeply, imagining a crystal blue light descending through all of your organs and all the way down through the bottom of your feet. Slowly exhale.... a crystal white light up through your feet, legs, abdomen, chest, throat, head and out through your mouth. Breathe deeply once again, bringing this crystal white light down through your body. Exhale this healing energy, and as you, do visualize your body glowing in a protective crystal white light of Divine Illumination.

Find yourself standing outside the gate of a beautiful Victorian garden. A gentle, warm breeze carries the fragrance of rose, lavender and peony through the garden, bidding you welcome. Breathe deeply the scent of these flowers, and as you do, feel their healing essence permeate your body.

1

Looking through the gate, you begin to see a brilliant, crystal castle off i the distance. As you focus on this magnificent dwelling, you begin to hear th celestial tones of a Stradivarius violin. Faintly at first, this music stirs your ver soul. Where have you heard this music before? What is the name of this piec and why does it touch you so deeply, so lovingly?

Suddenly, you hear someone very softly call your name. And as you look t see who bids you welcome, the garden gate begins to open gently. Steppin through the gate, the heavenly music of the violin becomes clearer, and althoug you see no one with you in this fantastic garden, you know that you are no alone. The fragrance of the flowers envelops your body. You feel safe and secure You feel loved.

Looking down at your feet, you see a rose petal covered path. What colo are the rose petals? Breathe in the scent of these rose petals. And as you exhale radiate the essence of these roses outward toward those you love.

You are drawn to the crystal castle that sits grandly at the other end of thi garden. What color is this divine dwelling? As you begin to walk the pathway you notice that the petals feel soft and velvety beneath your bare feet. Savor thi feeling.

Continuing on your journey you stop to take in the scent of the magnificen flowers that line the walkway. As you inhale their celestial scent, you feel you energy begin to rise. You feel rejuvenated. Stretching your arms upward towar the sun, you drink in its warmth and bask in the knowledge you are loved be-yond measure.

Again, you hear someone gently call your name. You know this voice. But, from where? When?

Following the sound of your name on the breeze, you realize that you have drawn close to the mansion. It seems to radiate a wisdom that speaks to you beyond your physical reality; beyond the past, the present or the future. It reso-nates with your very essence. Breathe in this wisdom and realize that you, too, embody the wisdom of the ages. And as you exhale, share this wisdom with those around you.

Approaching the marble staircase, you become aware of a bird perched on a branch just off to your right side. What does this bird look like? What does it have to say? Thank this creature for its message.

Ascending the twelve stairs toward the magnificent door of this castle, you hear the music of the violin becomes louder. As if by magic, the grand door swings open wide, revealing a scene unlike any other you have ever encoun-tered. You are standing in a majestic hall. The lone violin is now accompanied by a multitude of heavenly voices, and joined by symphony of divine instru-ments. The light of a thousand candles flickers as the scent of frankincense and myrrh fills your senses. You feel you have come home to a place you had forgot-ten, but one that remains with you throughout eternity.

As the music begins to soften and your eyes begin to adjust to the interior of this most holy place, a figure begins to appear. A light unlike any other sur-rounds it. It is the Light of Divine Love. As your celestial companion holds for-ward its hand in welcome, its dazzling wings begin to unfurl. Approaching this ngel, you notice the color of its robe. Notice, too, the symbol on the front of the ngel's robe.

Your Angel greets you with a warm, loving embrace. As you look into each ther's eyes, your angel speaks to you. It may be in symbols, it may be in a ingle word, perhaps more...Simply listen... What is his or her name? Listen vith your heart... What does this divine messenger have to say?

Your angel offers you a gift. It is a flower from the Garden of Divine Illumi- ation. Notice what kind of flower it is, for it shall remain a constant bond be- ween you and your Angel. Wherever and whenever you see this flower, it will be a sign from your heavenly companion that you are not alone.

Thank your angel for bringing you to this place and for sharing his/her nessage of love. As you embrace your Angel and then turn to leave, you are ware of the tremendous bond of love that is with you each day. A love that will emain constant throughout the ages.

Walking through the door and descending the marble stairs, you are greeted again by the bird singing on the branch. You feel whole and content. You feel oved. Breathe in this love and as you exhale, send it forth to those you love.

Once again, you feel your feet are upon the velvet rose petals. Winding hrough the Victorian Garden, you remember the music, the angelic choir, the warm embrace. You see your Angel's robes and the symbol upon the robes. You remember seeing your Angel,s eyes, and the wisdom they hold. Most of all, you remember the feeling of love beyond earthly measure.

You now find yourself at the garden gate. Looking back, you no longer see the crystal mansion beyond the flowers. It resides within you, where it has al- ways been. Feel the love of this place pulsate within your Being. Radiate this energy outward to those around you.

Very slowly and gently bring your focus back to your body, back to this room, remembering all you have seen and heard and felt. And when you are ready, gently open your eyes.

And so be it.

Reflections on Meeting Your Angels

What did you feel during the course of the meditation?

What colors, if any, did you sense? Did they take a particular form?

Were there any symbols that came to you? Draw or describe them.

What did your angel or guide look like?

Did he/she have a message for you? What was that message?
How was it delivered?

What kind of bird was present in the meditation? Were there any other animals?

Did they give you a message? How did they deliver the message? What was the message?

What color/kind of flowers were in the garden? Did they have a particular scent? What did this represent to you?

Did you hear any celestial music during the meditation? If so, how did it make you feel? What memories did it bring forth?

Following the meditation, what feelings are you left with?

The Enchanted Forest Meditation

 he purpose of this guided meditation is to encounter the Spirit of Nature. By embracing Mother Nature and all of the creatures who dwell within Her forest, we are nurtured and grounded. We feel a oneness with all life upon our planet.

Meditation: Breathe deeply. And as you do, gently close your eyes. As you exhale, release all worries, tension and anxiety. Relax. Breathe deeply once again, imagining a crystal white light descending down through your body and out through the bottoms of your feet into Mother Earth. Exhale this healing light, feeling it rejuvenate every cell in your body. Breathe deeply once again, imagining that you are surrounded in shimmering lavender light. Exhale once again, settling comfortably into your surroundings. It is a warm and sunny autumn afternoon. You find yourself at the edge of a magnificent forest, basking in the warmth of the sun's healing rays. Listen to the sounds of the forest. Breathe in its tranquil air.

Within these woods you sense a presence that beckons you forward. Perhaps it is an animal totem. Perhaps it is a nature spirit who wishes to speak with you and to enjoy your company. Listen. Listen with your ears, with your eyes and with your heart center. Breathe.

As you begin walking into the forest, the smell of autumn leaves and pine needles greet you. These warm and familiar scents fill you with a sense of whole-ess. You feel connected to Mother Earth and to those who inhabit her. The love the Creator dwells within this place. It dwells within the trees, within the powers and it is carried upon the gentle woodland breeze. Breathe in this Love and as you exhale, send it forth to those you love.

Journeying further into Mother Nature's magical forest, you come face to face with a magnificent tree. Never before have you seen such a large and majestic creature. You can feel the wisdom of this tree as it pulsates around you. Breathe in this knowledge and, as you exhale, send it forth to those around you.

The textured lines of the tree's ancient skin mesmerize you. It draws you closer. As you reach out to touch this magical timber, a face suddenly appears upon its bark. Looking into this face, you are drawn to the wisdom and compassion of its eyes. Look deeply into the face of this divine friend and breathe. Listen to the message that this noble nature spirit has to share with you. Watch as it speaks to you in the language of symbols. Listen as it speaks to you in the language of celestial sounds. Feel as it speaks to you in the language of emotion. Simply listen.... Now...Thank this Majestic Spirit for the message that it has shared. Thank it also for the gift of its protection and shade; for the many homes it provides to the four leggeds and to the creatures of the air. Thank the tree for its gift of oxygen and clean air.... As you turn to walk away, you place your hand once again upon its twisty, turny bark. You feel the love of this being pulsate in the palm of your hand. Return this feeling of love as you send warm heart chakra energy through your hand and into this majestic tree. With a smile, the face of the Nature Spirit begins to fade from view. You feel loved.

Walking back through the forest you feel energized and renewed. The sounds of leaves rustling under your feet and timberland creatures scampering across the woodland floor fill your heart with delight. The ancient and empowering energy of the forest leaves your Spirit soaring and your Soul refreshed.

Reaching the edge of the woods once more, you take a seat upon a log which lies in the meadow. Feeling the warmth of the sun upon your face, you remember the message of the Nature Spirit. You remember that you are connected to this place and to the One who created it. You feel Whole and you feel Loved. Breathe.

Now...slowly bring your attention back to your body, back to the sounds in this room. When you are ready, very gently and slowly open your eyes.

Reflections on the Enchanted Forest

What did you feel during the course of the meditation?

What colors, if any, did you sense? Did they take a particular form?

Were there any symbols that came to you? Draw or describe them.

What did the face upon the enchanted tree look like? What did the bark of the tree feel like?

Did this Nature Spirit have a message for you?

What type of animals were present in the in the Enchanted Forest?

Did they give you a message? How did they do so?

Were there any flowers, and if so, what color or scent were they? What did this represent to you? What kind were they?

Did you hear any celestial music during the meditation? If so, how did it make you feel? What memories did it bring forth?

Following the meditation, what feelings are you left with?

Guides Within the Temple

The purpose of this guided meditation is to connect with your Spirit Guides as you journey into The Temple Within. Our Guides in Spirit walk with us during our lifetime to help us accomplish our Soul's True Purpose. Some of our guides remain with us throughout our lifetime; some come into our lives to help us accomplish a specific task. This meditation will lead you to the Guide or Guides who are working with you during this period of your spiritual Journey.

Meditation: Breathe deeply through your nose. And as you do, settle comfortably into your surroundings. As you exhale through your mouth, send all worries, concerns and distractions away. Breathe deeply, imagining a crystal blue light descending through all of your organs and all the way down through the bottom of your feet. Slowly exhale.... a crystal white light up through your feet, legs, abdomen, chest, throat, crown chakra and out through your mouth. Breathe deeply once again, bringing this crystal white light down through your body. Exhale this healing energy, and as you, do visualize your body glowing in a protective crystal white light of Divine Illumination.

Find yourself in the majestic mountains of Tibet. The air is pleasantly cool as dawn begins to break over the horizon. Breathe in this healing air. Let it fill your body with rejuvenation and a sense of Divine purpose.

Feel the energy of the ancient trees and mountain plant life as they embrace your presence in this mystical place. These living beings will guide you as ou journey upward along the mountain path to the Temple of Illumination. The faint scent of cedarwood and frankincense begins to fill the air around ou. It seems to be coming from a temple that is barely visible in the distance. he trees, with their gnarly roots and ancient wisdom, beckon you to follow the rt path that lies beneath your feet. This path is the burnished red color of nnabar. You feel grounded and secure as you ascend the mountain.

Walking upward along the path, you sense a feeling of familiarity with our surroundings. You have been here before. Was it in a dream or perhaps a ast life? As you ponder this question, your Spirit is being gently pulled in the irection of the Temple. Off in the distance, you can see the Temple with greater larity. It is nestled in the morning mist. Smoke from the incense burning within he temple rises through the center of its ornate roof. You feel that someone is aiting for you within this temple, and you are flooded with a sense of love and onging for this person.

Along the path a small animal greets you. This creature conveys the mes-age that you are nearing the Temple and that all is as it should be. Thank this mall sentry for the message. Take note of this animal.

Breathe deeply the scent of the Temple. Exhale and as you do, radiate utward from your heart center, sending love to all living beings who reside on he mountain.

You are now approaching the steps outside the Temple. Looking upward ou see the orange and scarlet sun hanging softly behind this place of divine ontemplation. Slowly, you walk up the stone stairs. With each step, you are drawn further and further into the energy of the Temple. Within its walls you ense a familiar presence. You are happy and serene.

Upon entering the Temple, you are greeted by a thousand flickering candles, hat cast an amber glow about the darkness of this sacred place. The scent of rankincense and cedar fill your senses. Slowly, you remove your shoes and walk oward a silk meditation pillow that has been placed several feet from the front altar. As you look down upon this beautiful pillow, you notice a symbol embroi-dered upon this seat of reflection. Notice the symbol. Notice the color of the meditation pillow.

Take a deep cleansing breath and, as you do, gently seat yourself upon this meditation pillow. Exhale, knowing that you are safe and that you are loved.

As your eyes adjust to the candlelight, you begin to recognize someone seated in front of the ornately decorated altar. This Being is seated in lotus posi-tion. The wise and healing hands of this Guide are in gassho position as he or she finishes a mantra of prayer. Your sense of knowing tells you that this is the One who beckoned you up the mountain.

Breathe in deeply the Peace of this holy place. Exhale this mystical serenity to those you love.

While you gaze upon the figure of this celestial companion, your Spirit Guide begins to look up. Looking into their eyes you begin to remember. You have known this One, since the Beginning. Ask your Guide his/her name.

Your Spirit Guide has a message for you. Ask this Guide why you have been brought to the Temple. What is it that you came to find? To Learn? To

Experience? The answer may come in the form of a symbol, a single word, pe haps more. Listen. Listen with your inner ear. Listen with your eyes. Listen wi your heart.

As you both begin to rise from your seated position, look one more tin into the eyes of this Divine Companion. What do you see? Your Guide approach and embraces you. The warmth and love from this embrace fills your enti being. Remember this feeling. (short)

Descending the staircase and onto the pathway, you are again greeted t the small animal you encountered earlier. This creature nods in affirmation the magical experience you have just had in the Temple. He assures you that a is well. You are at peace.

Walk slowly down the mountain, basking in the warm sunlight and rejoi ing in the knowledge that you are always in the company of God's messenger Once again, see the symbol on the meditation pillow, the face of your belove guide and remember his or her divine message. Breathe in this tranquil air. Ho it for just a moment and exhale.

Very slowly, begin to feel your body. Begin to hear the sounds of this roon Bring yourself into the present. And when you are ready, very slowly open you eyes, remembering all that you have seen, heard and felt.

Reflections on Your Guides Within the Temple

What did you feel during the course of the meditation?

What colors, if any, did you sense? Did they take a particular shape or form?

Could you smell the incense burning in the Temple? How did it make you feel?

Were there any symbols upon your meditation pillow? Draw or describe them.
What color was your meditation pillow?

What did your Angel or Guide look like?

Did he/she have a message for you? How was the message delivered?

What kind of animal greeted you along the trail to the Temple?

Did it give you a message? How did It give you the message?

Were there any flowers, and if so, what color or scent were they? What did thi represent to you?

Did you hear any celestial music during the meditation? Could you hear the prayer mantra that your guide was reciting? What memories did it bring forth?

Following the meditation, what feelings are you left with?

The Angel Stone

he purpose of this guided meditation is to take you on a journey to meet your Angel. While in the Enchanted Garden, you will encounter the Brook of Angels where you will receive your Blue Angel Stone. This Celestial Stone will serve as a connection or conduit between your earthly home and the Angelic Realm.

Meditation: Breathe deeply and, as you do gently close your eyes. As you exhale, release all worries, tension and anxiety. Breathe deeply once again, envisioning lavender white light descending down through your body and out through the bottoms of your feet. As you exhale, feel this light rejuvenate and revitalize every organ in your body. Breathe deeply once again and, as you exhale, see this crystal lavender light surround your entire body and your aura. You are relaxed, you are grounded, and you are loved.

Find yourself in the middle of a lush and fragrant flower garden. The smell of roses, gardenia and lavender fill the air on this sunny, summer afternoon. The sunshine warms your face as you stretch your arms outward to receive its healing rays. You feel the soft and manicured grass beneath your feet. You feel childlike and playful as you wiggle your toes upon Mother Earth's thick green carpet.

Spotting a bench beside the babbling brook that runs through this magical garden, you decide to take a seat. Walking toward the bench, you encounter a small flock of butterflies with the most magnificent wings you have ever seen.

They seem to shimmer and glisten in the warm summer sun. As you gaze close
at them, you could swear they have human faces with human eyes. And, a
though you're not quite sure, it sounds as though they are whispering to or
another. You listen closely...Is it your imagination, or did you hear them sa
"They're here. They've finally arrived!"

Taking your seat upon the garden bench, you wonder, "Who has arrived
It must be your imagination...or is it? Settling comfortably upon the bench yo
are mesmerized by the relaxing sound of the water running over the stones i
the brook. The water glistens and dances in the warm sunlight. You feel relaxee
you feel grounded and you feel loved.

Gazing into the brook, you notice the most unusual stone that you hav
ever seen. This Celestial Blue orb reminds you of the sky on this beautiful clouc
less day. Rising up from the bench, you notice a slight breeze touch your checl
The fragrance of lavender begins to fill the air. Bending down now to reach fc
the heavenly blue stone, you are once again aware of the butterflies. They seer
to be hovering about in anticipation of something, but what?

Reaching into the cool waters of the babbling brook, you begin to hea
music. The sounds of violins, harps, cellos and mandolins seem to be coming ui
from the crystal clear water. Again, you hear faint, yet excited, whispers. Lister

When you hand finally reaches the Angelic Blue stone beneath the surfac
of the water, your entire arm and then body fills with a warm tingly sensation
You feel exhilarated. As you stand upright, with your precious blue stone betweer
your hands, you are amazed and awestruck to see an Angel standing before you

"I have been waiting for you, Dear One. We, of the Angelic Realm and Fae
Kingdom, welcome you."

Looking into the eyes of this Heavenly Being, you realize that you have
known this One before. Take note of the angel's robes or energy aura.

With hands outstretched, your angel offers you a gift. Take this gift. Wha
is it? Does your angel have a message for you? Listen. Listen with your ears
your eyes, your heart and your mind. Quietly listen.

Your Angel now speaks: "Dearest Child, Remember always that I am with
you. Call upon me and I shall respond. Listen for me in the sound of music or the
words of a song. See me in the flight of the butterflies or the movement of the
wind. The Angel Stone that you hold between your hands is not a mere rock, but
a heavenly creation, which links your earthly world with the Angelic Kingdom.
Call to me and listen; hold this stone and feel my presence."

Your Angel now takes the stone from your hand and holds it between his/
her heavenly hands. A mystical glow emanates from your Angel stone and from
the palms of your Companion's hands. Watch as your stone is imbued with
energy from the Angelic Realm.

Back in your hands, the stone now vibrates with an otherworldly energy.
Feel this energy and enjoy. This Angel stone is now your connection to your
Angelic Companion.

It is now time to bid your Angel good-bye for now.

As your Celestial Friend fades from view, you take your place once again
on the garden bench. You feel energized, you feel whole and you feel loved.

olding your Blue Angel Stone between your hands, you are aware that the owers in this wondrous garden are now more vivid, their fragrance more pro- und. You see things with greater clarity. You know that you are never, ever uly alone, and that your Companion is Spirit is but a dimension away. You joice in this knowledge, all the while basking in the afternoon sun.

Breathe deeply, remembering all that you have seen and heard and felt. xhale. Breathe once again, slowly, bringing your attention back to your body, ack to the sounds in this room and when you are ready, you may slowly open our eyes.

Reflections on the Angel Stone Meditation

What did you feel during the course of the meditation?

What types of flowers were in the garden? How did they feel? How did they smell?

Were there any symbols that came to you? Draw or describe them?

What did your angel or guide look like? What color was his/her eyes?

Did he/she have a message for you? How was the message delivered?

ow did the Angel Stone feel in your hands? Was it smooth or bumpy? Did you
el it vibrate?

Jhat color were the butterflies? Did their wings have patterns or designs?

)id they give you a message? What was the message? How was it delivered?

)id you hear any celestial music during the meditation? If so, how did it make
you feel? What memories did it bring forth?

Following the meditation, what feelings are you left with?

The
Temple of Isis

T he purpose of this guided meditation is to encounter the Egyptian Goddess, Isis, and to experience the healing energy of her Temple Isis is the Goddess of Healing and Renewal. Within her Temple you will encounter the sacred healing pool where you will be energized and revitalized within its healing waters.

Meditation: Find yourself on the banks of the, majestic Nile River. It is dusk. Torch lanterns are burning brightly along the waters edge as the Egyptian sun begins to fade on the desert horizon.   al and the Terrestrial, Mistress of Eternity. Isis.

Behind the grand columns of the Temple of Isis, you see firelight, signaling the start of the full moon healing ceremonies. It is time for you to make your way toward this mystical place, where hierophants prepare for this most sacred event.

As your journey toward the Temple of the Goddess, you feel the warm sand embrace your feet. You are connected to the Earth Mother. She envelops you in the wisdom of Her ways.

The scent Egyptian amber and sandalwood begins to fill the moonlight air as you approach this ancient dwelling of the Goddess. The aroma fills your being, and you feel peaceful.

Ascending the stairs, you are greeted by the High Priestess. Silently, she holds her hand out to you. Notice the symbol on the palm of her hand. As you

...ke her hand, she leads you to the center of the marble temple. Her silk robes glimmer in the candlelight. Take note of the color and texture of her sacred garments.

At the center of this Holy Chamber is a shallow pool of crystal blue water. This pool of Wisdom radiates with the healing energy of the Goddess Isis. The High Priestess invites you to sit near these healing waters with her.

Sitting comfortably upon the smooth marble floor, you find yourself gazing into the reflective waters of the sacred pool. Slowly, you are drawn further and further into these magical waters. Someone is beckoning you from within the pool.

Slowly a figure begins to appear. It is the Goddess Isis herself, who calls to you from Her home among the Stars. Gently, she smiles at you. The glistening water of the pool is reflected in her heavenly eyes as she invites you into the healing waters of Her Sacred Temple.

Wading into the knee-deep pool, you feel the warm healing waters begin to rejuvenate your Soul.

"What healing do you seek?" she asks.

Take a moment to reflect upon the healing that you seek. When you are ready, you may tell the Goddess of the healing you wish to receive. Remember to frame your question carefully, because you will receive what you request.

Take as long as you need to bask in the radiant healing which is now coming to you. Notice the color of the water and the way your body feels. Take note of any symbols or animals that may come forward. And enjoy.

The healing is now complete. You feel whole, grounded and at peace.

Thank the Goddess who stands before you for the healing you have just received. Isis embraces you and whispers a single word into your ear. Remember this word.

It is now time to leave this glistening pool.

The High Priestess returns to escort you back through the Temple. Taking your hands she leads to the steps of this majestic place. As you step through the column-lined entry, you are greeted by an indigo sky filled with a thousand brightly shining stars. The silvery light of the full moon caresses your body. Take a moment to bask in the Moon's healing embrace.

The High Priestess bids you farewell as you descend the marble staircase. Slowly, you walk the warm sandy path until you find yourself once again, sitting on the banks of the River Nile. You are peaceful, you are rejuvenated, and you are whole. Adonai, Adonai, Adonai.

And So Be It!

Now.... Slowly bring your attention back to your body and back to the sounds in this room. And when you are ready, very gently open your eyes.

Reflections on the Temple of Isis

What did you feel during the course of the meditation?

Did you feel the warmth of the desert sand beneath your feet? How did it make you feel?

Were there any symbols that came to you? Draw or describe them.

What did the High Priestess look like?

Did she have a message for you? How was the message delivered?

What did the waters of the healing pool like and feel like?

What did the goddess Isis look like?

What was her message for you? How did she convey her message?

Did you hear any celestial music during the meditation? If so, how did it make you feel? What memories did it bring forth?

What healing did you ask for? How do you feel following this meditation?

The Merkabah Meditation

The purpose of this meditation is to open your Merkabah energy field. Also known as the double star tetrahedron and the three-dimensional Star of David, this sacred geometrical energy field surrounds your body and your aura. It is your connection to the Divine and the Voice of Your Higher Self. When you open your Merkabah energy field, you are divinely protected and connected to the Source of All That Is.

Meditation: Breathe deeply through your nose and, as you do, gently close your eyes. As you exhale, release all worry, anxiety and troubles. Breathe deeply once again, visualizing a crystal white light descending down through your body and out through the bottoms of your feet. Exhale this grounding energy, feeling it revitalize every organ in your body. Breathe deeply one more time and, as you exhale, settle comfortably into your surroundings.

Find yourself sitting in the middle of a crystal clear pyramid. You feel energized, you feel safe and secure. Notice the rainbow colors being emitted from the pyramid walls. These wondrous colors envelope your body and your aura. Feel the energy of red (you are secure)…the energy of orange (you are creative)…of yellow (you are free to be who you intended to be in this lifetime). Bask in the energy of green (you are loved and give love)…the energy of sky blue (you are safe to speak your own truth)…and indigo (you see things clearly, through the eyes of unconditional love). Feel the energy of silver/gold and violet as it gently adiates around you. (You are connected to the Divine) Breathe in this energy and enjoy....

Your Spirit Guide now appears before you. Notice this Being.

Your Divine Companion now asks you to hold the palms of your hands out toward him/her. Your guide gently places a beautiful, radiating Merkabah crystal in your hands. Feel the energy of the celestial crystal beating in the palms of your hands. Watch as this double star tetrahedron begins to pulsate with all of the colors of the rainbow. Feel this Sacred Energy and enjoy....

Watch now as the Crystal Merkabah within your hands begins to grow larger. Still radiating the colors of the universe, this crystal clear Merkabah continues to grow until it completely surrounds you and your aura. You are energized, revitalized and divinely protected. Bask in the warmth of this three-dimensional Star of David, knowing that you are connected to the Universe and the Voice of Your Higher Self.

Your Guide in Spirit delights along with you as your Merkabah Energy Field pulsates with the rhythm of your body and the body of the Creator. Your Merkabah Energy Field is now open. Feel this energy field. It is real and it is powerful. It allows you to walk forward on your Journey, fully empowered by Universal Grace. Bask in this new awareness and enjoy.

Slowly now, bring your attention back to your body, and back to the sounds in this room. Breathe. And when you are ready, very slowly and gently open your eyes.

Reflections on the Merkabah Meditation

What did you feel during the course of the meditation?

Did you feel the colors being emitted from the pyramid walls? What did they feel like?

Were there any symbols that came to you? Draw or describe them.

What did your angel or guide look like?

Did he/she have a message for you? How was the message given?

ould you feel the Merkabah pulsating in your hand? What sensation did it give ou?

Vhat did the Merkabah energy field feel like as it grew larger and finally surounded your aura?

)id you hear any celestial music during the meditation? If so, how did it make you feel? What memories did it bring forth?

Following the meditation, what feelings are you left with?

The Orion Meditation

This meditation will take you to the Orion Constellation, where you will glide through the cosmos and make your fondest dreams come true. When we consciously co-create with the Universe, we begin a journey of abundance beyond our wildest imagination. And as they say, be careful of what you wish for...it just may come true!

Meditation: Breathe deeply. And as you do, gently close your eyes. Breathe deeply once again envisioning a violet crystal white light descending down through your body and out through the bottoms of your feet. As you exhale this violet crystal white light, feel this healing energy vitalize every organ in your body. You are balanced, you are grounded and you are whole.

Breathe deeply once again, releasing all tension, negativity and anxiety. As you exhale, see yourself surrounded by this violet crystal light. You are protected, you are safe and you are loved.

With this next breath, find yourself on a wooden stage, gently floating in the Orion Constellation. In front of you are thick, velvety, purple drapes. They are soft to the touch and radiate a loving energy unlike any other you have ever encountered. You are curious and excited to experience what lies beyond these curtains. Your body is tingly with anticipation as you wait for the golden cord to be pulled, revealing the other side.

A figure now appears. Avatar now stands before you. Avatar's robes are hite with a black vestment. You see the golden chalice upon his black vestents. This is the chalice of knowledge. From it flows the knowledge of the niverse. Also upon these holy vestments is a scythe with stars. This scythe cuts rough the ignorance in your life to reveal who you truly are.

Slowly, Avatar pulls the golden drapery cord, revealing the vastness of the rion Belt. You are left breathless at the sight of this cosmic wonder. In the close stance you see Mars. The message of Mars is: I am active. I am energetic. I am dependent. I am assertive. I am self-motivated. I am strong in body. Breathe in is magnificent energy from Mars. And Breathe...

Just beyond Mars you see Jupiter in all its brilliance. The message of Jupiter : I most enjoy growth. I most enjoy expansion. I enjoy success. I connect easily ith people. I am in touch with my Divinity. I am the wise teacher of all. I am umorous. I see the big picture. I make the most of everything that comes my ay. I hold truth as my highest value. Breathe in this wondrous energy from ipiter and enjoy. Breathe.

Beyond Jupiter lies Saturn. Watch Saturn as it slowly rotates within its plendid, protective rings. The message of Saturn is: I create useful forms for osterity. I manifest form. I create a structure that works. I have a healthy aware-ess of my limitations. I am disciplined. I learn my lessons. I use life's lessons for ny greater good. I am hardworking, conscientious. I set boundaries; I create oundaries. Breathe in this creative energy from Saturn and enjoy. Breathe.

Avatar now asks you to walk to the edge of the stage. Waiting before you is a large crystal disk. Upon the disk is the Universal Geometric Grid. Avatar now asks you to step out onto this celestial orb. Settle comfortably upon this disk as t carries you forward out into the Orion Belt. You watch in delight as you move past stars and see comets slowly shooting across the vast expanse. Notice the stars and comets. What color are they? Do they make any sound? Do they carry a message?

As you approach the center of Orion's belt, you see the Red Giant star of Betelgeuse shining yellow before you. The Blue-White star of Rigel shines off to your right side. In the Center of the Belt lies the Orion Nebula. This group of stars moves in a forward circular fashion, as if it were a fan belt or perhaps a treadmill. The magenta and royal purple stars glisten and glitter in the open sky. This is a magical place. It is a place of transformation and manifestation. Your crystal disk begins to slow as you approach the edge of the Orion Nebula. The radiance of this place fills your entire Being with Light and Love.

Avatar now appears beside you. Pointing to the center of the Orion Nebula, Avatar asks you to toss that which you desire to manifest, gently upon the Orion Belt, where it will be carried to the center of this powerful constellation and where it will be transformed into Reality. Watch as your desire is carried away among the stars and where it will be returned to you Manifest.

Your crystal disk now begins to make its way back through the Orion Constellation. You feel rejuvenated and energized as you gently float past Barnard's loop located at the sword of Orion. The bright red emission of the Rosette Nebula and the faint complex of the Cone Nebula seem to dance in the horizon. You are joyful and at peace.

Arriving back at the wooden stage, Avatar helps you from your crystal gr
disk and back on to the platform. Staring out over the constellation you feel
oneness with the Universe. You feel a part of All That Is.

Bidding you farewell, Avatar reminds you that your desires have been ca
ried to the center of creation where they will become manifest. He asks you i
look for the signs in the heavens. A shooting star, a speeding comet, perhap
one single star shining brightly in the clear evening sky. Simply watch and liste
as your intention becomes your reality.

The royal purple drapes now close once again. And you become aware c
your physical body, of the sounds in the room. Breathe deeply. And when yo
are ready, slowly open your eyes.

The planetary messages of Mars, Jupiter and Saturn are from:
Planetary Frequencies, Holographic Primary Patterns Book, by Chloe Faith
Wordsworth, 1995.

Reflections on the Orion Meditation

What did you feel during the course of the meditation?

What colors, if any, did you sense? Did they take a particular form?

Were there any symbols that came to you? Draw or describe them.

What did your Avatar look like?

Did he have a message for you? How did Avatar deliver his message?

What did the planets in the Orion Constellation look like?

What did Mars feel/look like?

What did Jupiter feel/look like?

What did Saturday feel/look like?

What desires did you toss upon the Orion Belt for manifestation?

What did your crystal disk look like? What did the geometric pattern on it look like? Draw or describe them.

Did you hear any celestial music during the meditation? If so, how did it make you feel? Did it bring forth any memories?

Following the meditation, what feelings are you left with?

Glossary of Symbols

Colors:

Pink: This is the color of love and of gentleness. It can be a reminder that you are loved and to be gentle with yourself.

Red: This is the color of the first chakra, which is located at the base of the spine. It represents safety and security. Red is a reminder to get fired up about life.

Orange: This is the color of the second chakra, which is located just below the navel. It represents creativity and intuition. Orange is a reminder that you are a gift to be shared with the world. Share yourself and your creativity.

Yellow: This is the color of the third chakra, which is located in our solar plexus. It represents autonomy and personal will. Orange reminds you that you are safe to be who you intended to be in this lifetime.

Green: This is the color of the fourth chakra, which is located in our heart center. It represents love. Green reminds us to love one another and to love ourselves.

Sky Blue: This is the color of the fifth chakra which is located in our throat center. It represents clairaudience, or clear hearing. Sky blue reminds us to speak our truth and to share our Truth with others.

Indigo: This is the color of the sixth chakra, located between our eyebrows in the center of our forehead. It represents clairvoyance, or clear vision. Indigo reminds us to see things clearly through the eyes of unconditional love. It is also a reminder to take note of what we see in our dreams.

Purple: This is one of the colors of the seventh chakra, which is located just above the top of our head. This chakra is our link to the Divine and the voice of our Higher Self. It represents our connection to the Creator and is the location in our energy system where Divine inspiration enters our energy field. Purple is the color of spiritual ity. It reminds us that we are never alone and that we walk in the company of Angels and Guides in spirit.

Silver: Silver is one of the colors of the seventh chakra. It represents high-vibration spirituality and our connection to God/dess.

Gold: Gold is one of the colors of the seventh chakra. It represents vibrations of the highest order in the realm of Spirit.

Sacred Geometry:

Merkabah: Knowledge, divine light. The merkabah energy field, which surrounds the human body, is used by the Master to connect with and reach those in tune to the Higher Realms. Also known as the double star tetrahedron and the three-dimensional Star of David.

Cube: Grounding and creation. Completion and foundation. Strength and the four directions. The cube represents Mother Earth.

Pyramid: This powerful formation represents a connection to the Divine; a gateway between the physical world and the world of Spirit.

Octahedron: Represents the Eight Paths to Enlightenment and the element of air.

Dodecahedron: Represents the twelve faces of the divine within.

Icosahedron: Represents the Kingdom, conscious prayer and the element water.

Sphere: Represents the circle of life and completion. For some, Angels and Guides in Spirit appear as spheres of light.

Tetrahedron: Represents Truth and Understanding. It is associated with the element of fire.

Symbols:

Ankh: This is the Egyptian symbol for life and health.

Sword: This symbol represents the "Sword of Truth" and the cutting away of the old to make way for the new. It also represents divine protection.

Chalice: This symbol represents the Cup of Knowledge, the Holy Grail. Perhaps your are being invited to drink from the cup of Divine Knowledge.

Elements:

Water: Represents spirituality and emotions. Perhaps you need to spend time near the water or take a long luxurious bath to get in touch with your emotions or spiritual self. Maybe a good cry is in order to release pent-up emotions!
If you encounter a river, you may be asked to get back into the flow of life.

Wind: The wind represents "the winds of change." New and wonderful adventures lie in store for you.

Fire: Fire reminds us to get "fired up" about life. It tells us to renew our interest in life. Fire may also represent the burning away of old-outdated beliefs and habits in order to walk confidently into the new.

Sun: Sun represents the energy of the Universe. It revitalizes and energizes us. It represents sunnier days ahead.

Earth: Mother Earth represents nurturing and a feeling of being grounded. She also reminds us of the Feminine Divine and our connection to all that inhabit Her.

Animals:

Bear: Awakening the power of the unconscious. Teaches you to go within and awaken your potential. Come out from your den and shine.

Eagle: Illumination of the spirit. Soaring to new heights. Eagle represents great sight and clarity.

Hawk: Hawk is the messenger and protector. It will lead you to your true soul purpose. When hawk shows up, pay attention. A message is coming forth from Spirit.

Crow: Represents magic, creativity and spiritual strength.

Turkey: Turkey represents the blessings of a successful harvest.

Deer: Represents gentleness. Be gentle with yourself and with others. Deer will gently lead you forward on your true soul path.

Raven: Represents magic and shapeshifting. Raven brings messages from the spirit world, and helps you delve into the darkness to bring forth your light.

Horse: Horse represents freedom and power. Horse will take you on brave new journeys and encourage you to ride in new directions.

Tiger: Represents the new moon and the full moon. Tiger reminds us to be passionate about life. If your life has become dull, tiger encourages you to awaken new passions in your life.

Rabbit: Represents creative manifestation, fertility and new life. Rabbit encourages you to manifest your heart's desire.

Mouse: Reminds you to pay attention to the details in your life.

Lion: Represents the Egyptian Sun God, Mithra, and the rising of the Female Sun. The lion is powerful and encourages you to bring forth new power, creativity and the use of intuition.

Dolphin: Represents the power of water, dreams, and intuition. You are being encouraged to learn proper breathing techniques and ancient toning in order to balance your physical and spiritual bodies.

Snake: Represents wisdom, transformation and healing. Snake represents death of the old ways and rebirth into the new. Snake encourages you to awaken your kundalini energy and get fired up about you physical and spiritual life.

Ascended Masters:

El Morya: Lord of the First Ray. A member of the Great White Brotherhood.

Lanto: Lord of the Second Ray. He teaches the ancient way of Universal Christhood.

Paul the Venetian: Lord of the Third Ray of Love. He teaches compassion, patience, understanding and self discipline. He encourages development of intuition and creativity.

Serapis Bey: Lord of the Fourth Ray. He represents the working of miracles.

Hilarion: Lord of the Fifth Ray. He represents healing and wholeness, music and science and third eye vision.

Lady Nada: Lord of the Sixth Ray. She represents the Holy Spirit's Sixth Ray gifts of diverse kinds of tongues and the interpretation of tongues. She oversees ministers, missionaries, healers, teachers, psychologists and counselors at law.

Saint Germain: Lord of the Seventh Ray. Represents the gifts of prophecy and the working of miracles. He is the High Priest of the Violet Flame Temple.

Maitreya Buddha: He is the Coming Buddha. Maitreya represents kindness, love, benevolence, friendship and goodwill.

Gautama Buddha: The Enlightened One. In his enlightened state he brought forth the Four Noble Truths which became the foundation of his teaching.

Jesus Christ: The Avatar of the Piscean Age. He is known as the Prince of Peace and the embodiment of the Word and the Universal Christ.

St. Francis of Assisi: God revealed to St. Francis the divine presence in "brother sun" and "sister " and rewarded his devotion with the stigmata of Christ crucified. People of all faiths throughout the world yet speak the prayer of St. Francis "Lord, make me an instrument of thy peace...."

Sanat Kumara: Revered in Hinduism as one of the sons of Brahma. He is the heirarch of Venus. He is the keeper of the three-fold flame of Life on behalf of Earth's people.

Kuan Yin: She is the Compassionate Saviouress of the East. Still very much a part of Eastern culture, Kuan Yin has awakened interest in her path and teaching among a growing number of Western devotees who recognize the powerful presence of the "Goddess of Mercy," along with that of the Virgin Mary as an illuminator and intercessor of the Seventh Age of Aquarius.

Mother Mary: Mary is the mother of Jesus Christ. Known as the Blessed Virgin, Queen of Heaven, and Mother of the World, she is a powerful ascended Master of great love, wisdom and compassion. She is an illuminator and intercessor of the Seventh Age of Aquarius.

Angels:

Metatron: Angel Most High. He is perhaps the greatest of all heavenly hierarchs. Metatron is the link between the human and the divine. He is the tallest angel in heaven.

Michael The Protector.

Raphael: The Healer.

Uriel: Divine Inspiration.

Gabriel: The Messenger.

Journaling the Journey
To
Your Temple Within